What are you doing this weekend to sell your book?

LCCN 2015932200

EAN 13-978-1507766767

ISBN 1507766769

 Your Time Publishing, LLC P.O. Box 872365 New Orleans Louisiana, 70187

Paula Tromp

What are you doing this weekend to sell your book?

A special thanks to:

My Teachers

Your Time Publishing, LLC P.O. Box 872365 New Orleans Louisiana, 70187

Table of Contents

22. Create Media Kit, choose colors, take photos, video
23. Platform
24. Who can you affiliate with?
25. Do some fact finding to verify compatibility with your platform.
26. Choose the top 5 most compatible. Collect contact data.
27. Develop joint ventures
28. Media blast
29. Author dossier
30. Issue 1st Press Release for milestones of finding an Affiliate.
31. Create a Business Structure
32. Set up business. Do all paper work
33. Accessories-Business cards, posters, sign for car
34. Advertising vs. Publicity
35. Develop side income
36. Understand financials
37. Determine price
38. Create Separate Social Network Accounts
39. Pinterest
40. Facebook
41. Twitter
42. Webpage
43. Linkedin
44. Blog

45. Schedule main release event

46. Media Contact List

47. Network

48. Make list of potential Book Reviewers

49. Solicit Testimonials – Make list of potential

50. Seek sponsors

51. Ask for referrals

52. Wrap up- Verify, Create Marketing Plan, and start selling

The time will pass anyway, you can either spend it creating the life you want or spend it living the life you don't want. The choice is yours.

If you are tired of starting over, stop giving up.

If you don't get what you want, it's a sign either that you did not seriously want it, or that you tried to bargain over the price. Rudyard Kipling (1865-1936)

The journey is the prize and every prize is the beginning of a new journey.

Learn to love all aspects of being an author.

Introduction

These tasks are from my own observations of skills needed and are inspired from the many marketing gurus and my own experiences of what it takes to effectively market your book.

So, you've written your best seller. Whether you have a traditional publisher, or you published yourself, or you have an e-pub only, the next task is to sell your book. The best advice one can give to authors is that they are responsible for selling their product. No publisher, distributor, or book store can sell your book to your target market the way that you can. Your target market will buy your book because you connected with them in some form.

This book was born out of the frustration seen on many authors' faces after the initial joy of receiving their first shipment of books.

How to use this book

This book has been designed to help you plan and manage the selling of your book. If you start at the beginning of your project to create a process, these are some of the tasks required to take your idea to the next level. This book will take you task by task, week by week to success. Documents have been developed so that you can verify that each task has been completed. Even if you have already begun your project, you can still utilize and accelerate these tasks. You do not need to complete tasks in the order presented and if you've already completed some tasks—this is great—just use the forms provided to document your findings. Some are simple tasks that can be completed in one sitting while others may take the entire week or longer depending on your personal schedule and your particular project. Understanding the scope of time constraints, the tasks have been broken down into weekly events. If you find or know that you have more time to devote to your project, you can accelerate the process. You can use this book as a reference for many projects or you can use it for a specific project. At the end, you will have enough information to build a solid platform, and business and marketing plans. From the information you accumulate, these strategies will catapult you to a solid foundation.

Once you've completed all the tasks you will have the material needed to begin the marketing and selling processes needed to create a bestseller.

You can use the forms supplied in this book, or you can use the format to create your own EXCEL book, or you can go old school and use a planner, or new school and find an APP that will keep you organized.

Thank you and good luck

Strategy

Prepare for your session

Schedule time

Use quiet physical space

Review tasks

Keep track

Complete tasks

Refine actions

Repeat

They say there is no magic wand to selling your product. I refute that theory. "The magic is in the plan and the follow through. Do something different."

Why use this book

Imagine if our forefathers (the average man) had not left us messages, such as, *The Bible, the Epic of Gilgamesh, En-hedu-ana's Hymns, or Instructions of Shuruppak.* What lessons we would have not learned. We need to continue to serve the future generations. You can, write that book, poem, song, to share with the world via blogs, journals, or books.

Me being a renaissance woman, I thought of all the different ways I could introduce this well worn topic to you in a fresh and comprehensive way. My talents lie in Publishing, Telecommunications, Music, Project Management, Art, and lastly Home Renovation. I take something from all of these disciplines as the sources to build a case. I believe that these experiences encompass the fundamentals necessary to accomplish the goals of creating the perfect plan, and the common ground here is PLANNING which is the key.

Week One

Success begins with the first task.

Setup tracking system

This task is the beginning of the process which will lay the foundation for your success as an author. In the appendix will be an excel book with pre-populated tabs. You can add as many tabs as you need. Take the time now to customize the spread sheets for your specific project. We're sure you'll need more calendar, note, and contact pages. Use these pages to monitor the progress of your weekly tasks, and to keep track of what you're doing and what needs to be done. Having your results all in one place will facilitate a positive outcome. At first, this may seem difficult, but once you set-up the system it will be invaluable.

Example of Excel spread sheets

Project Name:

Personal Contacts

Name:	Telephone:	email:	facebook:	Twitter:

Project Name:

Milestones:	Preliminary	Planning	Implementation	Evaluation

Notes:

Week Two

"The question isn't who is going to let me: it's who is going to stop me."-Ayn Rand

Ask yourself the right questions

<u>Types of questions</u>

Open ended (a non yes or no answer)

5 w's (who, what, where, when, why)

Probing (more information)

Clarify (understanding)

Closed (Confirm action)

Reflective

Pre-supposing (what if's)

Examples

How will you reach your target market?
What is your plan for selling your book?
What does the title of your book mean to you?
What about your book is interesting to the buyer?
Does the content have diverse market attraction?
Can you price the book to be affordable for target market?
Have you budgeted properly for this project?
What will it cost?
Is it suitable for other products?
Are you only relying on a distribution channel for selling activities?
Do you understand your responsibility to sell your book?
Is it marketed with perpetual (continuous) promotion?
Is your subject matter current and growing, or is your book seasonal?

What Are You Doing?

These are just a few questions. As you begin the process of understanding marketing, use your own situation to formulate specific questions for your project. As new questions come to mind, record them either in this section or in the section where they arise.

Notes:

Week Three

Success doesn't work unless you do.

Goals

- **S** - Specific (or Significant).
- **M** - Measurable (or Meaningful).
- **A** - Attainable (or Action-Oriented).
- **R** - Relevant (or Rewarding).
- **T** - Time-bound (or Trackable).
- **E** - Enthusiastic
- **N**- Natural
- **U**- Understood
- **P**- Prepared

Your first GOAL is to make a plan on how you're going to complete this book. Goals are the objectives that you want to meet. You will have more than one goal. Some examples of goals: finish writing the book, edit book, find an agent, or find a publisher. These are the goals for the writer in you. The goals we talk about in this book will be the goals to take your project to market. Actually, most of the weekly tasks in this book can be categorized as goals.

Example

Task - Design social networks

Specific- Choose colors, background, social networks, user ids, passwords

What Are You Doing?

Measurable- Have cohesive design so that branding is consistent and easy access

Attainable- Utilize available tools to obtain consistency

Relevant- This a is the foundation for the process of marketing

Time- bound- Allot one weekend to assemble this information

These have been added to the definition of the Goal SMART model to help the goal setter formulate an even better outcome.

- **E** - Enthusiastic
- **N**- Natural
- **U**- Understood
- **P**- Prepared

Project Name:

Goals

Specific	Measurable	Attainable	Relevant	Time Bound

Notes:

Week Four

Everybody has their strengths and weaknesses and it is only when you accept everything you are- or- you're not, that you will truly succeed.

Strengths/Weaknesses /Opportunities/Threats (SWOT)

SWOT analysis may be used in any decision-making situation when a desired goal has been defined.

Strengths: characteristics of the individual, business, project, or team that give it an advantage over others

Weaknesses: are characteristics that place the individual, business, project, or team at a disadvantage relative to others

Opportunities: *external* chances to improve your performance

Threats: *external* elements in the environment that could cause trouble for the individual, business, project, or team.

What Are You Doing?

Project Name:						
SWOT GOAL:						
Strenght	Weakness	Opportunity	Threats			

Determine your SWOT to understand where you need help.

- *Look at your goals and milestones.*
    - *Let's say you would like an interview on a local television station.*
        - *Strength*
            - *I wrote the book and did the research*
        - *Weakness*
            - *No prior interview experience*
        - *Opportunities*
            - *I'm being proactive*
        - *Threats*
            - *My knowledge may be challenged*

Notes:

Week Five

Good things come to those who wait or to those who get up and get it done.

Milestones

A milestone is a point in a project with a specific completion date that is considered essential to the overall completion to a project so that corrective actions can be taken and the goal can be completed in time. Each week can be defined as a task or a goal, any goal can be a task but not all tasks should be goals. The milestone should be significant and associated with a specific phase of the project (Preliminary, Planning, Implementation, or Evaluation). In addition to signaling the completion of a key goal, a milestone may also signify an important decision or the source of a critical piece of information which outlines or affects the future of a project.

- Preliminary-These are tasks that need to be completed in the beginning of a project.
- Planning-These are tasks that need to be completed in the information gathering stage.
- Implement-These are tasks that need to be completed during the execution phase.
- Evaluation-What were the key takeaways? Did you accomplish your tasks, goals, or milestones?

What Are You Doing?

Example

Project Name:

Milestones

Tasks/Goals	Action Date	Preliminary	Planniing	Implementation	Evaluation

Decide what is important to your success.

- o *Task/Goal*
  - ▪ *Finish weeks 1-13*
    - • *Choose a specific date*
    - • *Preliminary Phase*
  - ▪ *Complete Release Party Plan*
    - • *Choose a specific date*
    - • *Planning Phase*

Notes:

Week Six

*Be who you are and say what you feel because those who mind
don't matter and those who matter don't mind. Dr. Seuss*

Write questions for book and self

Know what type of questions you'll be asked. Listen to other interviews on
TV and radio, find questions online. Modify them for yourself and your
book. Use examples of questions that are always asked, then create
minimum 3, maximum 5 questions specific for yourself and your project.
Share information that will make your audience sense, experience, or
believe something. These are sample questions. Find or create some of
your own.

Example

- *What is your main message?*
- *How does this book help your readers or the community?*
- *If you had to give one final word on this book what would it be?*
- *Tell us something about yourself that your readers would be surprised to know?*
- *What is your motivation for this title?*
- *Do you have any writers' rituals, such as write at a specific time or when the
  mood strikes you?*
- *When/why did you begin writing?*
- *Why do you still write?*
- *What is your ultimate goal?*
- *What has been your greatest challenge, greatest victory as a writer?*
- *Who are your mentors and how have they helped you?*

What Are You Doing?

- *What do you enjoy most about the writing process?*
- *Most people have a picture in mind when they decide to become an author – did you? If you did, what was that picture?*
- *How do you develop your characters/storylines?*
- *If you have authored more than one book, which is your favorite and why?*
- *Do you have any more books planned in the near future?*
- *Why do you think we as a species write books?*
- *If you could have lunch with any author, who would it be?*
- *What advice would you give to writers who may be just starting out?*

Notes:

Week Seven

Let your faith be bigger than your fear.

Practice reading answers

Every time you speak to someone you are conducting an interview. Know how you want people to remember you. Make sure your message is clear.

Example

- *Practice in front of a mirror, on video and with others.*
- *Critique yourself and plan to improve.*
- *The goal is to get the audiences' attention and desire to purchase your product.*
- *Think about what would make you purchase a product?*
- *Go to a quiet room where you will not be interrupted.*
- *Set aside time every day.*
- *Practice talking into a cell phone and also a land line.*

Tips for Radio interviews

- *Research the show and tailor your message accordingly. Google the host's name and station and check out their web site. Is it a national audience or a small town? What is their format? Is it News/Talk, NPR or Classic Rock or something else? You need to know.*
- *KNOW exactly how much time you will have on the air as a guest, three minutes or 30 minutes...so you can tailor your answers to the time allotted.*
- *Practice your sound bites - out loud before the interview. Communicate your main points succinctly. Practice this out loud.*
- *Find a quiet place. Cut off all unnecessary electronics.*
- *Have a glass of water nearby; there's nothing worse than dry mouth during any interview.*

What Are You Doing?

- *Be self-assured. Remember, you know your topic inside and out. Be confident in your ability.*
- *Smile, smile, smile, whether on radio or TV - SMILE. You'll feel better, and for TV you'll look better too.*
- *Put pizzazz and energy into your voice by standing while you speak.*
- *Be informative and entertaining without directly pushing your book, product or service. Make the audience "want more."*
- *A kind word about the host can go a long way.*
- *A person's name is sweet music to them so commit to memory or jot down the name of the host and use it throughout the interview. When taking calls, use the names of callers too.*
- *Be prepared for negative comments, from the host or listeners.*
- *Be careful not to slide into techno-babble, jargon or acronyms that few know about.*
- *Never talk down to your audience.*
- *Be respectful of the host because everybody starts someplace. Today they're interviewing you from a college radio station; in a few years they could be a nationally syndicated host.*
- *Don't Oversell. Remember you are on the air to provide useful information to the listening audience. If you are an author or selling something, limit yourself to TWO mentions of the book, product or service. You must make it interesting without the commercialism. It takes finesse but you can do it. Often times the host will do this for you and you won't need to mention it.*
- *Think of a radio interview as an intimate conversation with a friend and not a conversation with thousands.*
- *Radio interviews require verbal answers, not head nodding or uh-huhs. Hand gestures don't count in radio either.*
- *Radio will often use interviews live and later cut them up for use throughout the day giving you more airplay. So keep your answer to a 10 to 20 second sound bite. You can say a lot in that amount of time and then you don't sound like you are babbling on. Don't go on more than a minute without taking a break.*
- *Don't just answer questions. Tell listeners something you want them to know, something they wouldn't know unless they were tuned in, with the promise of more of the same when they buy the product or come see you!*

What Are You Doing?

- *Have three key messages. Short, not sermons. Sometimes the host opens the door, other times you have to answer a question and segue to a key message. A compelling message will have the host asking for more. Usually people can get in two key messages; the pros can get three. But even if you get in only one, you get a big return for the time invested.*

- *Lazy hosts open with a lame: "Thanks for being here." Boom! Give a: 15-:20 sec summary message. If the host introduces you with a question, be polite, deliver your summary message, and then answer the question. "Thanks, (use name), for the opportunity to talk about....Now, to your question (name)..."*

- *Maintain a Positive Attitude. BE GENUINE OR TRANSPARENT. Don't fake enthusiasm or sincerity. If you're in a bad mood cancel the interview. Don't pretend to know stuff you don't.*

- *Re-read the press release or pitch that got the booking since the host is going to be using that as a starting point. Often a book publicist will tie into a breaking news event that relates to your expertise. Be aware of that tie-in.*

- *After the interview write a thank-you note. Since so few people do this, you'll really stand out from the crowd. And most importantly, you may get invited back.*

- *Whether the interview is live or taped-live, if you stumble, or flub up just keep going. Often what you perceived as a mistake, the listeners won't even notice.*

- *Ask for an MP3 of the recording before the interview. If you ask ahead of time the producer may record the interview and then you can use it on your web site. Be sure to listen to it later and critique your performance. You can always do better.*

- *Ask for a testimonial. The MP3 will arrive with a note from the host saying how much they enjoyed the interview, or that "you were a great interview, and really kept our audience engaged," or "the phones rang off the hook when you were being interviewed." You can use those testimonials in future pitches and on your web site, blog etc.*

Notes:

Week Eight

Be not afraid of going slowly; be afraid only of standing still.

Take this time to peruse the competition

Check Amazon.com/ Physical book Stores/Library/Specialty Stores

Example

- *You don't want to copy anyone*
- *But you also don't want to be too far off the norm*
- *Take notes*
- *Look for projects similar to yours*
- *See what others are doing*
- *Look at book covers*
- *Pricing*
- *Read reviews*
- *Read testimonials*

Notes:

Week Nine

At first glance it may appear too hard, but look again, always look again. —Rodmacher

Define your target market

Create Criteria to help you rank and organize your potential customers.

Identify your target market

It's crucial that you know exactly who wants your book. **List the benefits to each group of prospective customers. These are the reasons why the information in your book is important to them.** Am I your target audience, my son, my niece, my father or mother? If you don't know who your audience is, how can you sell them anything? A fitness trainer saying that his market is overweight people is not specific enough. Is it overweight men or women? By how much are they overweight? How old are they? What are their biggest challenges? What are their hopes for the future? Trainers use different methods for different people... and book sellers should do the same.

Some authors write from an unknown place, others write a deliberate subject. The one writing deliberate has an easier start because they know what they're going to write about and can envision who will buy their work. The author who writes from the unknown place usually has to see where the subject takes them in order to know who their target market will be. Ask yourself questions to find your ideal audience. Make some assumptions then test them to find your target market.

What Are You Doing?

Example

- *Who would want your book the most?*
  - *Either start with the largest or smallest group*
- *What makes you buy a product?*
- *Who do you think will buy your product?*
- *Why will they buy your product?*
- *Who are they?*
  - *Sex, age, education*
- *Where are they?*
  - *Demographics-city, sub, country*
- *What is their income range?*
- *Range of disposable income*
- *Sample Target Group*
  - *All woman*
  - *35-60 years of age*
  - *East coast*
  - *Urban setting*
  - *10,000 annual disposable income*
- *What can I do to sell my product?*
- *How will you reach them?*

Notes:

Week Ten

Faith is believing even wenh erveyhtnig loosk so wrong.

Where is your target market?

Every target market has a primary location where they can be found. You must figure out where they are so that you can share your message with them.

Examples

Where is your target market?

- *Schools*
  - o *Daycare*
  - o *Private*
  - o *Public*
  - o *Adult education*
- *Churches*
  - o *Denominations*
- *Book clubs Local and target area*
- *Book stores Local and target area*
- *Souvenir shops Local and target area*
- *Fairs and Trade shows*
- *Miscellaneous events*

Notes:

Week Eleven

Start by doing what is necessary; then do what is possible; and suddenly you're doing the impossible.

Make a list of all places in your immediate area that fit criteria.

Making lists and keeping track of the places where you can find your target market will help, especially as your region increases. You will use this information later to make contact and keep track of the results.

Example

Project Name:

Target Market Criteria Match

Location	Date Called	Address	City	Phone	Response

List Target Market Criteria Match

Research contact information

Notes:

Week Twelve

It's kind of fun to do the impossible. -Walt Disney

Make a list of all places in <u>surrounding area</u> that fit criteria.

Use spread sheet to collect data. Remember to get email and social network information. Note: you're still at the gathering stage so don't panic....

Example

Project Name:

Target Market Criteria Match

Location	Date Called	Address	City	Phone	Response

List Target Market Criteria Match

Research contact information

Notes:

Week Thirteen

Some people dream of success while others wake up and work hard at it.

Compile data

Names of locations, address, telephone, email, website, contact, etc.

- *Use Excel spreadsheet, calendar or contacts to create your own personal phone book with your list of contacts.*
- *Prioritize in what order you will begin to make contact. Start with the local and smallest groups first.*

Project Name:

Target Market Contacts

Name: Telephone: email: facebook: Twitter:

Notes:

Week Fourteen

Life isn't about finding yourself. It is about creating yourself.

Create logo for self

- *This is not a mandatory task*
- *This logo is for you the author vs. for the business you are going to create.*
- *You may need to hire this step out but definitely have some input.*
- *Use local college student (this can help spread your message)*
- *This is good for Branding yourself*

Examples

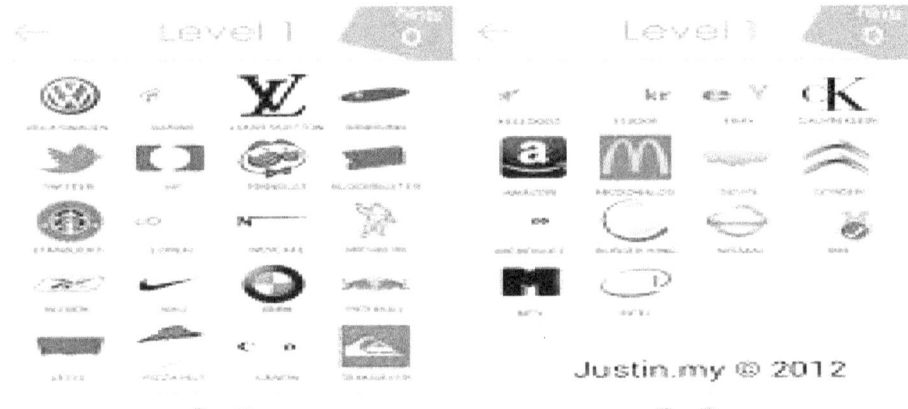

Justin.my © 2012

Project Name:

Logo

Notes:

Week Fifteen

Imagination is more important than knowledge.

Choose title

You can start with a working title but start thinking and working toward your final title. The title like everything else is a marketing tool. You want it to be as interesting as your book in order to entice your target market to purchase your product.

Examples

Beloved by Toni Morrison

Devil in a Blue Dress by Walter Mosley

Harry Potter by J.K. Rowling

Green Eggs and Ham by Dr. Seuss

Act Like a Lady, Think Like a Man by Steve Harvey

Fifty Shades of Grey by E.L. James

HerStory:Revelations by Paulette Jones

Notes:

Week Sixteen

Start where you are and do what you do.

Synopsis

Synopsis- for every chapter there should be a paragraph-who, what, where, when, how. Below is what is expected by agents and publishing companies.

Example

- *Use a 1-inch margin on all sides; justify the left margin only.*
- *Put your name and contact information on top left corner of the first page.*
- *Type the novel's genre, word count and the word "Synopsis" in the top right corner of the first page.*
- *Don't number the first page*
- *Put the novel's title, centered and in all caps, about one-third of the way-down the page.*
- *Begin the synopsis text four lines below the title.*
- *The text throughout the synopsis should be double-spaced (unless you plan to keep it to one or two pages, in which case single-spaced is OK).*
- *Use all caps the first time you introduce a character.*
- *After the first page, use a header on every page that contains your last name/your novel's title in all caps/the word "Synopsis": Name/TITLE/Synopsis.*
- *After the first page, number the pages in the top right corner on the same line as the header.*
- *The first line of text on each page after the first page should be three lines below the header.*

Notes:

Week Seventeen

Every possibility begins with the courage to imagine.

Elevator speech

This is your opportunity to share your story with every contact you make. When people ask you what you do or who you are, you will have a prepared speech. You will have practiced this speech so much that you will even have your facial expressions down to a science.

Example

30 second

My Name is _____. I am the author of _____. It is about_____. It is a task by task guide with example, charts and spreadsheets. There are 52 individual tasks to be accomplished each weekend or to accelerate the process the tasks can be worked as time permits.

1minute

My Name is _____. I am the author of _____. It is about_____. It is a task by task guide with examples, charts and spreadsheets. There are 52 individual tasks to be accomplished each weekend or to accelerate the process the tasks can be worked as time permits. I started this project because…Add more

Notes:

Week Eighteen

Life always offers you a second chance. It's called tomorrow.

Biography

In your final biography add published author.

Example

Mary Wells, a native of New Orleanian, started writing at John McDonough High School. She went on to Journalism at UNO. She worked for the Times Picayune for five years before embarking on a career as a fiction writer. After Hurricane Katrina, Ms. Wells has become a Lifetime Member of New Orleans Coast Fiction Workshops. Ms. Wells recently completed her Master's Degree in Literature from New York University, and is currently pursuing a Writing Fellowship to Stanford University. This is her first published novel, and her goal is to be a Noble Prize of literature winner.

Notes:

Week Nineteen

Life is not about waiting out the storm it's about learning to dance in the rain.

Cover design

- Associate to something familiar ex. human face
- Make a mock up of your book cover
    - placement of author name/title
    - choose colors
    - typeface/fonts
    - images
    - be cognizant of white space
    - back cover narrative
    - short author bio
        - Mary Monroe is the third of four children, born in Toxey, Alabama. She spent the first part of her life in Alabama and Ohio, moving to Richmond, California in 1973. Successful author and mother of two children, Mary currently resides in Oakland, where she continues to write bestselling novels.
        - J.K. Rowling (b. July 31, 1965, in Chipping Sodbury, England) became an international literary sensation when the first three installments of her Harry Potter children's book series took over the top three slots of The New York Times

best-seller list. The phenomenal response to Rowling's books culminated in 2000, when Harry Potter and the Goblet of Fire became the fastest-selling book in history.

- ○ self picture

Examples

Notes:

Week Twenty

Today you are you, that is truer than true. There is no one alive who is youer than you! - Dr. Seuss

Article about self as a writer

Not just your biography. Share as much personal info as you're comfortable with. Tell a funny or interesting story.

Example

My name is Shade` (Shaw-day, like the Jazz singer) Johnson. I'm a twenty-five year old graduate from the English department at Columbia University ('14), the founder of my own non-profit organization (www.succesforkids.org), and the former reigning Miss Orange New York. When I found out that Diabetes was the number one killer of African Americans aged 25-44, I knew that Diabetes awareness would be my platform for the year. Recognizing that if people are dying in the middle of their lives of Diabetes then they are contracting Diabetes in their teens and twenties, I targeted high schools for Diabetes prevention messages. I became the Diabetes Project's Youth Ambassador for Diabetes Prevention, arranged for mobile testing units to visit parts of New York with little or no access, and spoken at high schools all over New York City.

I was honored by New York City's Mayor Bloomberg's New Artist Award, for "capturing the spirit of the Diabetes awareness movement," but was most excited to present my experience as an advocate in public schools before Congress in hopes of writing curriculums for nationwide disease education.

As my reign came to a close, I realized that Diabetes awareness wasn't just a campaign platform or some cheesy beauty queen "issue of concern," it has become a passion for my life and I hope to one day be a part of major policy changes in our country's education systems. I'm currently awaiting decisions from public health graduate schools. But long before the woman who seems so presentable now, was a high school drop-out whose promiscuous behavior landed her in a drug treatment facility. I had lost all sense of who I was, validating myself in my dysfunctional, unhealthy, and often unprotected encounters. Looking back, I know I was searching for my father in men who could never replace him. But even deeper than that, I think I was struggling to find a definition of myself without the man who had helped to build my identity.

Notes:

Week Twenty-One

And those who were seen dancing were thought to be insane by those who could not hear the music. -Neitzsche

Article about book

Fiction-Choose a section of book and put a beginning and an end then submit as a selection for an article.

Example

- *Readers Digest*
- *Magazine excerpts*

Non-Fiction-Choose the top three points of your book and write everything you know about them.

Example

- *If book is about finance*
  - *Saving*
  - *Investing*
  - *Credit*
- *If book is about playing guitar*
  - *How to tune guitar*
  - *How to hold guitar*
  - *How to strum guitar*

Notes:

Week Twenty-Two

Use your smile to change the world, but don't let the world change your smile.

Create Media Kit, choose colors, take photos, video

The media kit, like all of your marketing, should be uniformed in colors and other aspects. We used PowerPoint to create the example below, but you can use Publisher, Word, or even only video if you choose. We included, author biography, press releases, partial audio interviews, pictures, video, book description, and cover. This will be used when a media source requests more information about author.

Example

  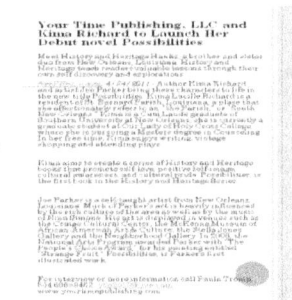

Video Process

The planning phase	Sound design
Story boarding	Editing
Writing the script	Delivering
Graphics, Illustrations and animations	Promoting
Voice Over	

Notes:

Week Twenty-Three

Believe there is good in the world.

Platform

Creating a platform is not just the art of friending people on facebook or twitter or even a large email contact list. People buy books or other products because they FEEL something from you or your product.

A writer's platform means having a niche, a hook, a theme. Something you believe in. What do you want to be known for? You could be like a television personality who wants to help others be their better self, or a spiritual leader who wants everyone to know of Jesus' love for us, or a financial maverick who wants us to be responsible for our finances.

Once you name your platform, you will be able to influence groups of people to spread the word about you and your book. Just as books are sold to your readers through bookstores—which are essentially entities with influence and large followings—you can communicate through people who are interested in your cause and who have large networks and who will now have a reason to support you.

What Are You Doing?

Once your platform is defined these are some influential groups that might be of assistance.

- *Good friends.* They could be your classmates, fellow employees, relatives and neighbors. This is probably the weakest category in terms of their desire or ability to spread the word about your book.
- *Centers of influence.* Who are the well-known people that can influence the purchasing decisions of large groups of your target readers? These could be celebrities, industry icons, people in the media, or bloggers with a large following.
- *Professional associates.* People who have a following in a specific niche can spread the word among their constituents.
- *People in your affinity groups.* Find and participate in groups of people with similar interests or needs and who know you personally.
- *Fans.* These are people in your target audience who have read your previous material or have heard you speak on your topic. They believe that you know what you are talking about and are willing to put their reputations on the line by becoming your advocate.

Notes:

Week Twenty-Four

I may not be the strongest, I may not be the fastest, but I am trying my best.

Who can you affiliate with?

Associate yourself and book with an existing group or person who is representative of your platform; this person or group will help spread your message. You are five contacts away from anyone you might want to reach. Learn the name of the first of those five people. The goal is to have them become your advocate. Networking face to face with each contact will bring you closer to your goal. Conduct your personal networking activities wherever people congregate. You can target specific places where your prospects are most likely to be, such as those listed below. First define who they are, then assemble a list of the possibilities.

Examples

- *Associations. Go to a directory of associations such as the one at weddles.com. Sort the list to find those most applicable to your topic and visit their websites. Find the staff and board members and make contact with them. If there is a local chapter, attend a meeting and ask to be a speaker at a future meeting.*
- *Personal presentations. Speak before groups such as Rotary Clubs, Chamber of Commerce meetings, trade shows, libraries, corporate meetings or at schools.*
- *Trade Shows. Hundreds or thousands of industry people -- including media people, potential customers, suppliers and networking contacts -- congregate at appropriate expositions looking for new products, information, contacts and ideas. Find relevant shows to attend at biztradeshows.com*
- *Attend seminars. Learn more about your topic and network with people there.*

- ***Perform events at retail stores.*** *Do not attempt to simply conduct book signings. Instead, hold events that promote you as the expert on your topic.*

Notes:

Week Twenty-Five

Keep away from people who belittle your ambitions. Small people always do that, but the really great ones make you feel like you can be great too.-Twain

Do some fact finding to verify compatibility with your platform.

Your personal networking will be more productive if you use common sense and courtesy. Do not overload people with information, but do conduct a friendly conversation for a mutually beneficial exchange. Your objective is to help them understand how your book can benefit them, as well as the people in their reference groups.

Once you have your foundation in place, continue building your platform among people who could buy your book. Use mass-communication techniques to generate a large quantity of contacts. Then when your core group connects with them, your potential buyers will recognize your name and book title. Use the internet and other media strategically to reach as many people as possible on a regular basis.

Notes:

Week Twenty-Six

Nothing is more exhausting than the task that is never started.

Choose the top 5 most compatible. Collect contact data.

Use Excel spread sheet notes pages to collect data about persons or groups, read and understand their mission statements and biographies. Compare and choose best fit.

Example

Project Name:					
Affiliates					
Contact Name	Date Called	Address	City		Response

The STAIR organization is a volunteer-based, non-profit children's literacy organization that provides reading tutors for public elementary school students.

If I write children's books, they might be a good fit.

They've been in the local area for 25 years.

They might have many contacts in your field of expertise.

Notes:

Week Twenty-Seven

Go confidently in the direction of your dreams! Live the life you've imagined.-Thoreau

Develop joint ventures

Brainstorm and strategize about participating in an event that your target market, affiliate, or anything relating to your platform is having, or develop a program that you can participate in. Strategize for win/win prospect.

Example

- *Speak at an event about your message*
- *Have a booth at a conference*
- *Have a book discussion*
- *Give discount coupons/certificates to a complementary business*
- *Co-sponsor special events and promotions*
- *Co-sponsor with a non-profit organization*
- *Affiliate programs*

Notes:

Week Twenty-Eight

The most effective way to do it is to just do it.

Media blast

A media blast is a one page informative sheet about some event, milestone or goal reached. This would be sent out to your email list.

Example

"Katrina: One Set Of Footprints" is the second adult novel from author Paulette Jones. This book is an account of how Paulette and her group of family and friends end up in the mist of Hurricane Katrina. It is a testimony that GOD is real even in the middle of a storm. Paulette writes this not to explain the reason for this book:

"I wrote this XXXXXXX. I was inspired to write after XXXXXXX The most significant and probably my favorite thought from the book is XXXXXX

Paulette Jones' charismatic approach to reality sets her apart, she's a savvy business woman who "represents the new era author and brings a new and bright perspective to authorship, as she entertains and enlightens us with her witty collection of thoughts and inspirational language." Publishing Company, LLC

Notes:

Week Twenty-Nine

Don't be afraid to fail.

Author dossier

This is used to send to media and others, such as an affiliate, or sponsor.

Example

FEATURED GUEST EXPERT:
Please contact this Guest Expert to interview her on your show!

Shadé Ashani, Author, is encouraging others to seek their power and strength through realization and revelation.

Your listeners may or may not be ready to hear this story, but if they are like most folks, they are not ready to ignore the facts.

In her **new book** *In Search Of My Father*, find out how the loss of our fathers' physical presence or negligence impacts and shapes us.

In sharing her story she reviews the epidemic of sexual assault in our country and how issues like **"PTSD"** and absent fathers compound the problems. She discusses the topic of untreated sexual assault and the resulting depression then encourages women to seek treatment; 1 in 6 women are raped before the age of 25 and these are only the women who report. She envisions her story to be a wave of healing over an increasingly fatherless nation.

"PTSD" is a hot buzz word in psychology circles, especially as more of our veterans come home from war. If your listeners want to have a better understanding, they can find out where one can go to get help.

In Search Of My Father encourages everyone to participate in their life planning to be the best people, partners and parents.

Book Shadé Expert and Author to discuss.....

- The effects of sexual assault
- The signs and symptoms of **"PTSD"**
- The changing demographics of American families
- Why people fathers are needed now more than ever
- How faith can play a major role in the healing process
- Mandatory steps individuals and families must take to solidify our place in the world
- Starting a new plan for how we want to live
- Shade's book, *In Search Of My Father.*

Shadé Ashani Guest Expert Interview Credentials

- Shadé Ashani is sharing her life story, her memories only as she can recall.
- Shadé has always been creative, a story teller, a scholar, a healer.
- Shadé believes there is a plan for all of us that through prayer, faith and education will be revealed .
- Author of *In Search Of My Father*

Notes:

Week Thirty

Wake up every morning with the thought that something great is about to happen.

Write sample Press Release for milestone of finding an Affiliate

A press release is information supplied to reporters: an official statement or account of a news story that is specially prepared and issued to newspapers and other news media for them to make known to the public. There are several online sites that will allow you to fill in the blanks then they will format and distribute your press release. See appendix for sample press release.

Example

Send out PR whenever there is a milestone such as:

- *Sign contract with publishing company*
- *Affiliate with non-profit group*
- *Final edit*
- *Release date of book*
- *Events-book readings/signings*
- *Lectures/discussions*
- *Release Party*

Notes:

Week Thirty-One

Live as if you will die tomorrow; learn as if you'll live forever. - Gandhi

Create a Business Structure

Name your Business, business type-sole proprietor, design logo, state license, letterhead, PO Box, Federal Tax id, Business plan, Mission statement, bank account, etc.

Marketing and selling a book is business. Creating a business will give you tax advantages. If you set up a company for the sale of your book, you will be able to deduct many costs that are associated with the process. Even the purchase of this book can be deducted.

Examples

- *What R U Building Enterprises*
- *Sole Proprietor/ Partnership/LLC/Non-profit/Corporation*
- *City License-Occupational License*
- *LA309 or 396 to Reserve Business name and then to register Business name*
- *EIN -Federal Tax ID form SS4*
- *Business Plan/Mission Statement*
- *PO Box from USPS or private PO Box*
- *Bank Account*
- *Get general ledger*
- *Other…*

Notes:

Week Thirty-Two

You are always stronger than you think you are.

Set up business. Do all paper work.

Once the decisions are made the proper forms must be filed with local, state, and federal agencies as well as banks, post office, etc.

Examples

- *Occupational License*
- *Business type:*
    - *Sole Proprietor*
    - *Partnership*
    - *LLC*
- *Federal Tax ID*
- *Chase Bank*
- *US Post Office*

Notes:

Week Thirty-Three

If you find a path with no obstacles, it's probably not worth traveling.

Accessories-Business cards, posters, sign for car

Examples

Vista Print or Local Printer

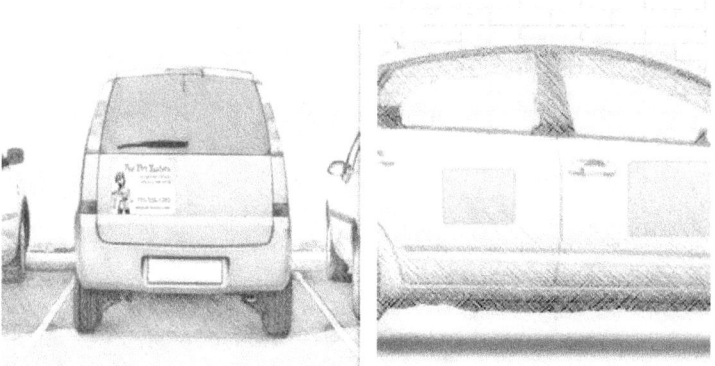

Notes:

Week Thirty-Four

Give people more than they expect and do so cheerfully. -H. Jackson Brown, Jr.

Advertising vs. Publicity

Look at adverting in magazines and online to see what could work for your project.

Example

1. *Advertising- usually COST$$*

   - *Newspapers*
   - *Magazines-have longest lead time*
   - *Special directories*
   - *Theater and other event programs*
   - *Calendars*
   - *Sponsorships*
   - *Special events*
   - *Sports teams*
   - *Cable TV/Local Access*
   - *Radio*

2. *Publicity – package so people want to share your message-Usually NO COST*

   - *Press Releases*
     a. *Announcements (moves, hires, contracts)*
     b. *Brags (awards, appointments, achievements)*
     c. *Special Events (seminars, speeches, appearances)*

   - *Publicity Events*

    a. *Related to seasonal celebrations*
    b. *Local festivals*

- *Column*

    a. *Local newspaper*
    b. *For corporate publications*
    c. *For professional journals and trade association newsletters*
    d. *Church or community newsletters*

- *Radio Shows*
- *TV shows (cable/local access)*

Notes:

Week Thirty-Five

Don't stop until you reach the stars.

Develop side income

Such as t-shirt, tutu, apron, jump rope, posters, dolls, journals, candles, cups, glasses, tote bags, etc.

Example

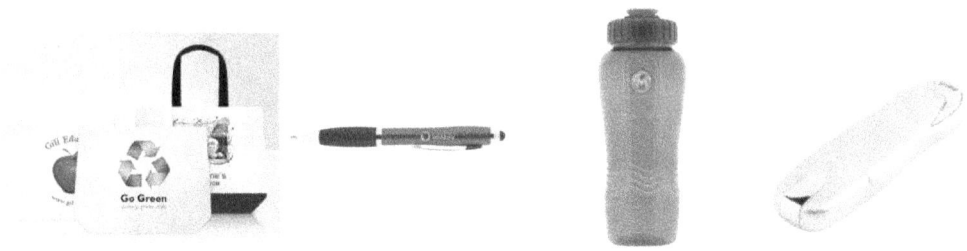

Notes:

Week Thirty-Six

When you want something you never had, you have to do something you've never done.

Understand financials

These are common numbers an author needs to know: 40/60 split is usually what the distributor or direct sales to book store will contract for, 50/50, 30/70, 7/7/86, these are other splits that can be negotiated between publishers, other distributors and e-book publishers. Publisher contracts vary but range from 7-10%, they will sell you books at a 30-50% discount, e-books may compensation you with 65-75% of retail price. These numbers are approximate and negotiable between all parties.

Example

- *Know your margins*
- *Most 3rd party sellers will expect a 40/60 split*
- *Your contract will state your royalty payments*
- *Keep track of payments*
- *Money Tree*
  - *Advance*
  - *Passive (royalties)*
  - *Bulk Sales*
  - *Licensing*
  - *Additional customers*
  - *Website*
  - *Referrals*
  - *Free Publicity*
  - *Additional Revenue*
  - *Speaking Engagements*

Notes:

Week Thirty-Seven

You will come to know that what appears to be a sacrifice will prove instead to be the greatest investment that you will ever make. - Hinckley

Determine price

Look at what the books in your genre are selling for, what are your costs and what profit would you like, also, if you have a publisher they will probably weight in on this subject. Most publishers will allow you to purchase your book at a discount, usually about 50% off retail.

Example

Harry Potter $25.99 hard cover/ 13.99 trade @ 50% discount

If your book is retailed priced at 13.99, then your purchase price per book would be $6.995. There may be other charges such as shipping or taxes. Assuming a 20% cost for miscellaneous cost that would add 1.399 for a total cost 8.394 leaving a profit of 5.596 per book.

If your book is retailed priced at 25.99, then your purchase price per book would be $12.995. There may be other charges such as shipping or taxes. Assuming a 20% cost for miscellaneous cost that would add 2.599 for a total cost 15.594 leaving a profit of 10.396 per book.

Notes:

Week Thirty-Eight

If you can dream it, you can do it.-Walt Disney

Create Separate Social Network Accounts

Consider how you want them to look, be uniformed. Link networks together so that you will have easier access for updates. Choose the SNA's that will best reach your target market. New Social Network sites are probably created every day, so if one is not listed here their site will tell you how to use. Ex. Instagram

Example

Book Title as user logon, make password relevant, and choose colors or same background for all systems.

Project Name:

Social Networks

SNAccount	UserID	Password	Fonts	Colors

Notes:

Week Thirty-Nine

Do all things with love.

Pinterest

Many authors are finding creative ways to promote their books using the social scrapbooking site. Millions of people currently use Pinterest, and that figure is climbing fast; some data shows that Pinterest is the fastest growing standalone website ever.

What exactly is Pinterest?

Pinterest is a combination of a digital pin-up board and a scrapbook. It's a bit like Twitter, only for pictures and videos instead of 140-character tweets. From your Pinterest page you can create different boards for different interests– one for book covers, one for photos of characters in your book, one for pictures of you and your readers, one for photos of your writing desk, etc. Plus, other people can pin things to your page (if you allow them to become "contributors" to a particular board), which encourages more sharing and interaction.

How authors can use Pinterest as a promotional tool

Well, if you've spent much time on social networks, you know that shouting "Buy my book!" every couple days is a sure way to annoy your followers. You have to be more subtle, more sideways, and more creative. Pinterest is a great way to enhance your author "brand," build your platform, and create compelling content that supports your book promotion efforts. And since Pinterest users can create unlimited "boards" for each new interest or topic, you've got options.

Examples

- *Create a Pinterest board for the main characters or settings in your book.* Ask your fans to add photos they think help make those people and places feel real. What does the mysterious hero look like? What about pictures of that icy field where the murder took place? (Note: you'll have to add these fans individually as "contributors" to that particular board before they can pin their own content to it).
- *Give us a behind the scenes glimpse into your process.* Show fans your desk, your typewriter or computer, your waste basket of discarded poems, the view outside your window, etc.
- *Get aspirational.* Where do you want to travel on your book-tour? Where would you love to spend a week writing? Show us the photos!
- *Ask for inspiration.* You can create boards to bring your previously created characters into 2D. But the process can flow the opposite direction, too. What about asking your readers for help when you're just developing a new story? Are you searching for the right details about pistols to put into your Western? Ask for some photos of old guns.
- *Promote your friends and heroes.* Social media followers are turned off by constant self-promotion, but pimping books by other folks can go a long way. You're giving solid recommendations to your fans, and the writers you promote will be thankful.

Some basic rules for using Pinterest

Again, if you've been using Facebook or Twitter for a while, the same general guidelines apply to Pinterest.

What Are You Doing?

- *Stay engaged in the conversation.* Don't just post your own content and call it good. You need to re-pin, like, and comment on other people's Pinterest content. Follow the Pinterest boards of writers you admire.
- *Put the "P" symbol on your site* or blog so your readers will know they can also follow you on Pinterest.
- *Make sure the names of your boards have catchy titles.*
- *Large photos are best.* Pinterst is all about the visual. Pick great pics.

Notes:

Week Forty

Don't let anyone ever dull your sparkle.

Facebook

Facebook Author Page

You should be talking about your writing on your personal profile just as you talk about other aspects of your life, but there are some good reasons why you should make the leap and take the focused promotion efforts off of your personal Facebook profile and create a Facebook page dedicated to your literary pursuits.

First we need to clear up a little terminology. Facebook calls the typical individual profiles **Personal Profiles** and they refer to the profiles created by a brand, product, organization, musician, or writers as **Profile Pages**. It can get confusing as they can look similar, but there are some big distinctions in how they work. Also, you must have a Facebook personal profile first before you can create a profile page, so if you're new to Facebook, you'll have to create that first. Once you're up and running with a personal profile, here is how you can create a profile page.

Examples

- *Go to this link http://www.facebook.com/pages/create.php*
- *Select the Artist, Band, or Public Figure button*
- *Once that is selected, you will get a drop down menu where you will want to select "author"*
- *Enter your author name in the "name of page" field and click create page.*

What Are You Doing?

- *Now that the page is created, be sure to post a profile image and a "cover image" (the large banner-style photo across the top) and drop your bio and press into the info section.*
- *Once you reach a certain number of Fans (Some say it's 100, but we've seen it work with fewer), you can set a username for your page. This creates an easy to remember Facebook URL http://facebook.com/YOUR-USERNAME. Just go to http://facebook.com/username to create the URL for your page.*

Notes:

Week Forty-One

Open your mouth only if what you are about to say is more beautiful than silence. -Arabic proverb

Twitter

Think about how you'll use twitter. This is a place you can create interest in your project. Use this sight to share with your followers the progress you're making. You can *retweet your* press releases or media blast. Talk about your characters or locations. If you have a non-fiction book, share tips from your book.

Example

Break your story up and tweet it in chunks.

Tweets can only be 140 characters long, which means you can't include every detail of your story in one tweet. Break your release into "chunks" and tweet it out over a period of time. That will extend your news cycle and give people more chances to notice your story and retweet it with their own networks.

Use #hashtags to tweet your news to more people.

When tweeting your story, categorize it by adding a hashtag (aka the 'pound sign') to a word or phrase relating to your story or industry. As well as getting you seen by people outside your network of followers, it will put you on the radar of journalists and bloggers who are interested in or following that hashtag.

Newsjack.

Is there a current event or trend that relates to your brand or a piece of news you've put out recently? Tie your story into the bigger trend and tweet a summary, using the appropriate hashtags to get your tweet into the conversational mix.

Blog your news, then tweet it.

Make your news release go further by writing it in a different editorial format. By inserting a little opinion and perspective, you can turn your news into a blog post. Perhaps you can include a customer example or a relevant anecdote that will make the news even more relevant to readers of your blog. Then, promote your blog post via Twitter. This is a great way to keep followers interested by presenting a new angle on the same story.

Create a video.

How excited about your news are you? Why not show people by recording a short (one minute, max) video of you announcing your own news, and tweeting the link? Video is a good way to convey a little more emotion and show off the human side of your business — and it's also very shareable on social media.

Becoming a part of people's Twitter conversations can get your news to the readers who really care about it, and it shows that you want to engage with them. Remember: If you're going to promote your news release on Twitter, make sure to do it in the context of what your audience is interested in, and balance self-promotion with plenty of engaging conversation.

Notes:

Week Forty-Two

She believed she could, so she did.

Webpage

Your publisher may give you a webpage or you can create one with GoDaddy, WordPress, Webs, or some other free site, or of course you can purchase one. You can again use this site to keep in contact with your clients and share useful or entertaining information. You can also sell your product directly from some sites.

Example

Get Your Website Online Easily

With all of the hats you wear managing your business, getting a website up and running can seem a little overwhelming, but it's easier than you think. The basics you need to get started

- *Choose a good website name*
- *Choose a website provider*
- *Cost-effective options for building your site-many site builder programs are free*
- *The 3 C's of a successful website*
  - *Consistent*
  - *Content*
  - *Contact*

Notes:

Week Forty-Three

Follow your heart, believe in your dream, and create your own reality.

Linkedin

LinkedIn is the world's largest professional network with millions of members and growing rapidly. LinkedIn connects you to your trusted contacts and helps you exchange knowledge, ideas, and opportunities with a broader network of professionals. There are many groups already built into LinkedIn. Search for your target groups, affiliate groups, business groups.

Example

The first step to success on LinkedIn is writing a compelling and complete personal profile. Use this format to create.

How To Use LinkedIn Keywords ....
Your LinkedIn Headline ....
Uploading a Photo ....
Writing a killer Summary ....
Skills and Expertise ....
Your Exsperience ....
Contact Information and Website Links ....
Education...
Honors and Awards ....
Interests ....
Advice for Contactacting...
Projects ....
Adding Images, Videos, and Documents...
Thanks! ....

Notes:

Week Forty-Four

> *Nothing great was ever achieved without enthusiasm.*

Blog

How to Start a Blog

Blog hosting. Which type is right for you?

There is web hosting and then there is *blog* hosting. This is hosting that is specifically designed for blog users, providing them with the features they need to maintain an appealing and interesting blog. These features include multimedia files, video and images which can all be used on the web host's servers. Because most websites use some kind of blogging platform, most website owners opt for the service of blog hosting, simply because it is an extra service that provides so much more in terms of hosting.

There are two types of blog hosting: Self hosting and remote hosting. Remote hosting means that the contents of your blog will remain under the control of the blogging platform. Popular platforms including Blogger.com and WordPress.com are extremely popular among bloggers today and to choose them for remote hosting is a good idea. Remote hosting can be great for personal blogs as it takes care of all the design and maintenance hassles.

There are however a few problems with remote hosting if you are using a blogging platform for professional purposes. Because your content is controlled by these free sites, there could be problems beyond your control. For example, if the site decides to shut down, your blog and all of its content can be lost forever. Furthermore, if you want your blog to appear professional, it is not recommended that you have an address ending with the words 'blogspot.com' or 'wordpress.com'. It will appear unattractive to future investors and it is best that you spend some extra money on a self hosted site which will look more credible.

The advantages of self hosting far outweigh remote blog hosting. You have the option of totally controlling the look and operation of your blog without the limitations imposed by free blogging platforms. If you choose blog hosting with a well known web hosting company, they will be able to offer you endless benefits for your blog such as SEO and extra traffic benefits. Many hosting companies also offer multiple blogging platforms as part of their hosting packages. This is useful if you want different themes to support your particular blogging needs.

How to find the best hosting for your blog

If you want to get your blog up and running in no time, it is recommended to browse through some of the best web hosting companies and see what they have to offer in terms of blog hosting features. If you are new to the world of blog hosting, you should opt for a company that offers easy installations. All you need to do is choose your domain name and your hosting company will take care of the rest, providing you with a professional looking blog on some of the best blogging platforms.

Notes:

Week Forty-Five

Success is not the result of spontaneous combustion. You must set yourself on fire.

Schedule main release event

> If you are planning a main event for your book launch, start planning minimally eight weeks before event.

Example

Depending on choice of venue, you may need more lead time. Celebrating and discussing your book can happen in a variety of ways. Here are some suggestions based on what other people have done:

- *Set up book discussions at library branches throughout the city with librarians serving as moderators. A Discussion Guide can function as an outline for these meetings.*
- *Give a lecture or participate in a "town meeting."*
- *If the author is unavailable, invite another writer who has been influenced by the author or an expert on the author's writing to discuss the book and the issues it addresses.*
- *Set up a re-enactment of a key section of the book with a local theater troupe.*
- *Set up a "town meeting" with prominent local figures discussing the book.*
- *Work with local restaurants or coffee shops to host discussion groups in their locations.*

The involvement of other sponsoring groups in the Community-Wide Reading Program may open unique promotion possibilities, but the following suggestions should work in nearly any town:

- *#1 priority should be to work with all media contacts to garner as much print and broadcast coverage as possible.*

What Are You Doing?

- *Give posters and postcards to local schools, businesses, churches, temples, and any other organization that wants to support the initiative.*
- *Provide local bookstores with promotion material that can be used to build displays in the stores. Ask the local bookstores to feature the book in their newsletters and on their Web sites.*
- *Advertise the title selected and the programs in the local paper. Note: Advertising costs can dramatically increase the budget of the program unless another party is underwriting the advertising.*
- *Run announcer read ads on the local public radio station.*
- *Run excerpts from the audio-book edition on the local public radio station (with the publisher's permission).*
- *If the author is involved in the events, set up interviews with the author on local television and radio programs prior to public appearances and events.*

Notes:

Week Forty-Six

You are confined only by the walls you build yourself.

Media Contact List

You will create this list and use it to request interviews and other types of support. Keep track of who you spoke to, when you contacted them, and all other pertinent information. Ask if you can send more information; if yes send Media Kit or Author Dossier.

Example

Project Name:

Media Contacts
Date Contacted

Contact Name	Date Called	Telephone	email	facebook	twitter	Response

Notes:

Week Forty-Seven

The people, who are crazy enough to think they can change the world, usually do.

Network

Example

- *Contact anyone you've ever had any business or social interaction*
- *Create email to send*
- *When you send emails make sure to use BCC*
- *Create a 1min spiel to people you need to call.*
- *Promise yourself to attend an event every month*
- *Make a new contact*

Project Name:

Network Contact

Contact Name	Who shared contact	Telephone	email	Response

Notes:

Week Forty-Eight

Telling the truth and making someone cry is better than telling a lie and making them smile.-

Make list of potential Book Reviewers

When seeking reviews, be prepared to send out a copy of your book along with a headshot photograph, author dossier, and information on where your book can be purchased. This is when you would mention your wonderful new website!

How do I find a reviewer?

- *Google book reviews or reviewers.*
- *Look at books similar to yours to see who reviewed them then Google for contact information.*
- *Ask all fans to review your book either at Amazon, Barnes and Noble or even on your website.*

Project Name:

Book Reviewers

Name	Date sent	Telephone	Address	City	Response

Notes:

Week Forty-Nine

Do not settle for less than exactly what you want.-Durbin

Solicit Testimonials/ Endorsements

Testimonials (sometimes called "blurbs") are statements by people attesting to the quality of writing and the value of the content in your book. They offer objective support of the prospect's buying decisions, that his or her money will be well spent. If you can get celebrities to endorse your book, the positive impact on the prospective buyers will be greater, and consumers will be more likely to buy it.

Famous people can be believable endorsers, but not all feelings about celebrities are positive. Some can actually have a negative effect on people who do not like them. And if the celebrity places himself or herself in a negative situation during your promotional campaign, the fallout may impact your sales, so choose wisely.

Example

How to Get Endorsements from Celebrities

Obtaining endorsements from celebrities is not a difficult task. The key is to make it as easy as possible for them to reply. Your request should include a cover letter, a copy of your book and a self-addressed-stamped envelope (SASE).

In your email or letter to them, include your table of contents and chapter titles and a galley copy or sample chapters. Let them know you are aware of how busy they are, and send a list of words and phrases from which they can choose. You might say something such as, "Other readers said something like this ... ." Ask if they would like to have you write the testimonial for them.

Shoot high. Before you ask for a blurb, ask the VIP to write the introduction or foreword to your book. Most people will be flattered to have you ask them to write it, but will probably turn you down. Acknowledge that you recognize the time pressures on the person, and then offer to write the section for him or her. If they still decline, then ask for the blurb or offer to write it for them.

Getting a good endorsement or testimonial can take time, but if you do not hear back from them in two or three weeks send a follow-up letter or email. Celebrities are busy people, and often their mail is screened by an assistant, delaying your request from getting to them. Where do you find the names and contact information for these VIPs? Here are some general sites on which you can begin your search.

1) The Screen Actors' Guild (www.sag.com). SAG represents nearly 120,000 actors in film, television, industrials, commercials and music videos. Contact SAG at 5757 Wilshire Blvd. Los Angeles, CA 90036-3600; (323) 954-1600. You can ask for a list of agents at (323) 549-6733. If you are on the East Coasts contact SAG at 360 Madison Avenue, 12th Floor, New York, New York 10017, (212) 944-1030.

2) Another free list of addresses, contact information and important tips on how to reach celebrities may be found at http://www.reelclassics.com/Address/address-list.htm

3) A site with free background information about celebrities is http://www.who2.com/

How to use your blurbs

Place blurbs on the rear cover of your book. Also use them in your sales literature, in your press releases and press kits, on your website, on book marks, in your advertising and on sales-promotional items. If you have a powerful endorsement from a top celebrity or a recognized industry expert, place it on the front cover of your book.

Resist any temptation to rephrase your customers' words. That will generally lower the believability factor. But if a testimonial goes over two or three short sentences, it may be too long for people to read and grasp its meaning quickly. In this case, extract a short phrase that characterizes the essence of the blurb and use only that. Never try to misrepresent the intention of the endorser. According to the Federal Trade Commission (FTC) "The endorsement message need not be phrased in the exact words of the endorser, unless the advertisement affirmatively so represents. However, the endorsement may neither be presented out of context nor reworded so as to distort in any way the endorser's opinion or experience with the product. Endorsements must always reflect the honest opinions, findings, beliefs, or experience of the endorser."

Always seek and record positive comments about your book. Get permission from the providers and use their blurbs generously in your marketing material. You will gain credibility through your association with these people, and your sales should improve as a result.

Notes:

Week Fifty

Please and thank you are still magic words.

Seek sponsors

Make list of best persons to contact. Between your target group, affiliate, and platform information find businesses that are in tune with your messages and request a sponsorship for some event that you are involved. See sample sponsorship letter in appendix.

Example

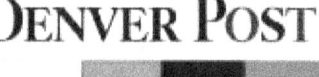
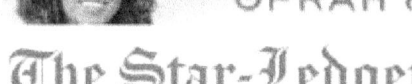

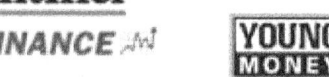

Corporate Sponsors:

_____

_____

_____

_____

Non Profit Organizations:

_____

_____

_____

If you can find the connection between yourself and an existing organization, it will help get you where you want to go. You can borrow the credibility of the organization you're associated with and can profit from their PR and Media. This will decrease the time and effort and the cost may be deferred to the larger group.

The best person to contact at corporations is

_____.

The best person to contact at nonprofit organizations is

_____.

Notes:

Week Fifty-One

Nothing that's worthwhile is easy, remember that.

Ask for referrals

Example

Everyone you meet from this point on is a potential customer or contact. Use this new found super power to open up a whole new world. Whenever you are given the opportunity to share your story ALWAYS ask if they know anyone they think would be interested and would it be ok to use them as an introduction.

Project Name:				
Referrals				
Contact Name	Date Called	Contact info	Who Referred	Response

Notes:

Week Fifty-Two

In the end we only regret the chances we didn't take.

Wrap up-Verify, Create Marketing Plan, and start selling

Preparation is the key to your success.

After completing this program, you will have the tools and information needed to develop a Marketing Plan. You know and understand your product. You have complied all of the reasons someone will want your product. You know where they are. You have a platform that is relevant and timely. You have found the people who are likely to help you. You have written the dialogue that needs to be used to share your message and have practiced to the point of competency. You have complied all that you need to be successful and now you know how to add or subtract ideas. You will use all the data you've gathered to create a marketing plan.

What is a marketing plan?

The Marketing Plan defines all of the components of your marketing strategy. You have addressed the details required to create a market analysis, sales, advertising, customer service, implementation plan, public relations campaigns. Focus Social Media to a few networks. This will be your one year plan to be analyzed on a monthly basis.

Marketing Plan Outline

I. Executive Summary

This section will be completed last and will summarize the information you've accumulated for the Marketing Plan from the information gathered during of the weeks of WRUD. Include ownership of company, biography of author, copyright of book(s), information about market and industry, any guaranteed distribution or contracts, your products (books and side products), and will include the platform information.

II. The Challenge

This is the description of your book and how it will be marketed, and the associated goals. You will include information from weeks 3, 4 and 8, 13, 23-24, 27, 45.

III. Situation Analysis

This section analyses the business you've established to sell your book, your target market, your competitors, and your potential collaborators. The below mentioned weeks will have information for this section.

Company Analysis-weeks 3-4, 31

- Goals
- Focus
- Culture

- Strengths
- Weaknesses
- Market share

Customer Analysis-week 9-13

- Number
- Type
- Value drivers
- Decision process
- Concentration of customer base for particular products

Competitor Analysis-weeks 4, 8

- Market position
- Strengths
- Weaknesses
- Market shares

Collaborators-weeks 23-27

- Subsidiaries, joint ventures, and distributors, etc.

SWOT Analysis-week 4

A SWOT analysis of the business environment can be performed by organizing the environmental factors as follows:

- The company's internal attributes can be classed as *strengths* and *weaknesses*.

- The external environment presents *opportunities* and *threats*.

IV. Market Segmentation

Present a description of your target market segmentation as follows: weeks 9-13

Segment 1

- Description
- Percent of sales
- What they want
- How they use product
- Support requirements
- How to reach them
- Price sensitivity

V. Marketing Strategy

Discuss why the strategy was selected, then the marketing mix decisions (4 P's) of product, price, place (distribution), and promotion.

Product-weeks 14-19

The product decisions should consider the product's advantages and how they will be leveraged. Product decisions should include:

- Brand name
- Quality
- Scope of product line
- Warranty

- Packaging

Price-weeks 8, 36-37

Discuss pricing strategy, expected volume, and decisions for the following pricing variables:

- List price
- Discounts
- Bundling
- Payment terms and financing options
- Leasing options

Distribution (Place)-weeks 23-24, 27, 34

Decision variables include:

- Distribution channels, such as direct, retail, distributors & intermediates
- Motivating the channel - for example, distributor margins
- Criteria for evaluating distributors
- Locations
- Logistics, including transportation, warehousing, and order fulfillment

Promotion-weeks 24-30, 34-51

- Advertising, including how much and which media.
- Public relations
- Promotional programs
- Budget; determine break-even point for any additional spending
- Projected results of the promotional programs

VI. Short & Long-Term Projections

The selected strategy's immediate effects, expected long-term results, and any special actions required to achieve them. This section may include forecasts of revenues and expenses as well as the results of a break-even analysis. Weeks 3, 35-37

VII. Conclusion

Summarize all of the above.

Exhibits

Calculations of market size, commissions, profit margins, break-even analyses, etc.

Notes:

Appendix

Press Release-is a written or recorded communication directed at members of the news media for the purpose of announcing something newsworthy. format: Word, PDF

Media Kits-is a collection of information pertaining to a particular person or entity, may contain photos, press releases, biography, video, etc. format: MSPowerPoint, PDF

Author Dossier-a file containing detailed information on a particular person. format: Word, PDF

Book Synopsis- is a brief summary of the major points of a written work, usually as prose but could be in a table. At least a paragraph for each chapter. format: Word, PDF

Sound bites- Audio files of your interviews, trailers, readings. format: MP3, podcast, wma, wav

Video- Video clips of interviews, trailers, readings. format: Youtube,wmv,mp4

 Project Phases:

>   Initiation

>   Planning

>   Executing

>   Controlling

>   Closing

Personal Marketing- selling yourself
Social Network- on line friends and contacts
Personal Network- off line contacts
Website- online presence
Publicity- the sharing of information to increase public awareness
Media- means of communication, radio, television, newspaper, or magazines, with wide reach and influence
Blogging- a website that displays postings in chronological order with links for posting comments

What Are You Doing?

Awards-American Literary Awards and recognition
Events-Literary events, Sponsor events
Festivals- Local, State book festivals

Contact: Name
Publishing Company, LLC
Phone 504 XXXXXXX

P.O. Box, XXXXXX
New Orleans La. 70187

**Publishing
Company, LLC**

Press Release

Publishing Company, LLC, Releases, Author's Name first novel *What are you doing?*

New Orleans La, July XX: Publishing Company, LLC announces the release of Author's name new book, *What are you doing?* invites us to a place most of us could not even imagine. It strolls around the Bayous of Louisiana and then tosses us into the more modern enclaves of New Orleans suburbs. There's something for everyone on the pages of this unfathomable tale of wealth, power, lust and love. Author's name, a native New Orleanean, was first recognized when three of her stage plays were performed at the Black Repertory Theater in Berkeley, California in the early nineties. *What are you doing* is her first non-fiction book. For more information go to: www.publishingco.com.

# # #

Publishing Company, LLC is an independent publishing house. Publishing Company, LLC goals are to be a global leader in the field of general interest publishing, dedicated to providing the best in fiction and nonfiction for consumers of all ages, across all printed, electronic, and audio formats. For more information, visit our website at http://www.publishingco.com/

Sample Sponsorship letter

Name   Name of Recipient:
Address   Name of Organization:
New Orleans, La. 70187   Address: Airline Hwy
Telephone   City: Metairie, La.
email   Phone Number: XXXXXXXXX

Date: 11/29/20XX

Sponsorship Request

Dear Sir/Madam

I am writing to see if <u>Contact name</u> and <u>Business name</u> would be interested in sponsoring the book launch event for local author, <u>Author name</u>. Her book, *Book Title,* published by *Publishing Company* will be available at local bookstores as well as online at Amazon, Barnes and Noble, and Books-a-Million and other local businesses. A portion of all sales will be donated to <u>one of your Affiliate Organizations</u>, (Get mission statement from your contact person or their website if available.) which is *a non-profit organization dedicated to reversing the plight of children in our community through recruiting, training and supporting an army of volunteer mentors throughout the metropolitan area. Amidst the devastation of violence, drugs, teen pregnancy and crime in our community today, the future appears grim unless we, as individuals and corporations, act decisively to effect positive changes and offer concrete alternatives to this generation,* and the national (place another organization if you have one)FFAWN organization, Foundation For the Advancement of Woman Now, which started as a dream to inspire women from all walks of life to gain the confidence and skills they need to reach their individual potential. Publishing Company and Author both see these organizations as partners in the building of lives, will you join us. All donations will be made in the names of our sponsors.

What Are You Doing?

This event is scheduled for January 9, 20XX from 6pm-9pm at Name and address of venue, Orleans, Louisiana 701XX.

Author name a New Orleans resident has written a book that promotes self motivation and personal growth for all women who seek refuge in literature. Tell a little about book and its value to the community and any other pertinent information about target market. The target audience is women between the ages of 21-34; secondary target group is ages 15-20 and of course we believe all women could benefit from this book, New Orleans total targets are 113,324 per 2008 Census Bureau ACS with a median income of 29,193. 64.

Share information about event. We are using this venue to honor 20 local business women, who are leaders in the community and have excelled in their careers. They will share with us some of the adversities they have endured and conquered, these are the images we want to share with the young women of the charities we support. We want to create a tradition of showcasing positive role models for today's young women.

We are requesting sponsorship for this event from local businesses and would be grateful for your assistance. Having your company partner with us for this event would be a natural match because of your standing in the community and your desire to promote positive images.

We are seeking help specifically with: bouquets of pink roses to honor the 20 women and for decorations, clear 6" plates, clear silverware, white napkins, hot and cold cups and any other thing that you can share. We expect 200 guest, list who will be attending, and who has been invited, Publisher; and other guest will be our speakers. Some of the women invited are XXXX. Media will be invited to broadcast this open event. We will place banners recognizing all sponsors and names will be included on programs, website and all social networks.

Thank you for your time and consideration

Name of Author

www.ingramcontent.com/pod-product-compliance
Lightning Source LLC
Chambersburg PA
CBHW081215280526

45787CB00006B/2414